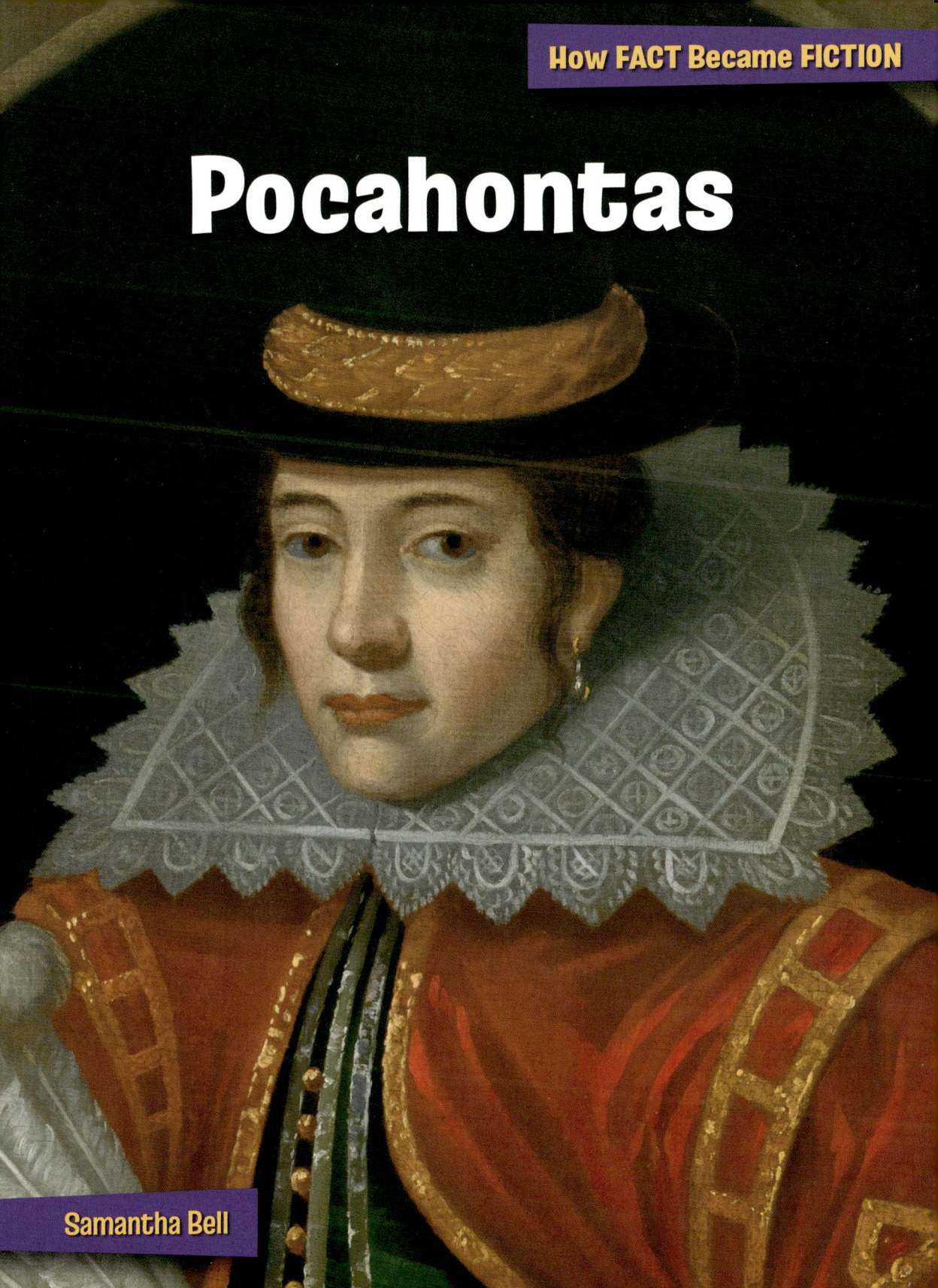

How FACT Became FICTION

Pocahontas

Samantha Bell

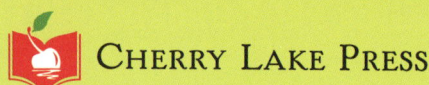

Published in the United States of America by Cherry Lake Publishing Group
Ann Arbor, Michigan
www.cherrylakepublishing.com

Reading Adviser: Beth Walker Gambro, MS, Ed., Reading Consultant, Yorkville, IL
Content Adviser: Heather Bruegl, M.A. (Oneida/Stockbridge-Munsee) Historian-Indigenous Consultant-Lecturer

Photo Credits: cover: National Portrait Gallery, Smithsonian Institution; transfer from the National Gallery of Art; gift of the A.W. Mellon Educational and Charitable Trust, 1942; page 5: John Henley/National Park Service; page 6: Houghton Library, Harvard University via Wikimedia Commons; page 7: Sidney E. King, U.S. Geological Survey; page 8: © Visharo/Shutterstock; page 9: Library of Congress; page 11: Lithography of Powhatan's mantle, Ashmolean Museum, Oxford, 1888. Image cropped from plate XX of Edward B. Tylor, "Notes on Powhatan's Mantle, Preserved in the Ashmolean Museum, Oxford." Internationales Archiv für Ethnographie, volume 1 (1888), pages 215–217, via Wikimedia Commons; page 12: © MRoald/Shutterstock; page 13: © Bob n Renee/Flickr.com (CC BY 2.0); page 14: © Tony Campbell/Shutterstock; page 15: Carol Highsmith/Library of Congress; pages 16–17: Library of Congress; page 19: Wikimedia Commons; page 20: National Portrait Gallery, Smithsonian Institution, gift of Betty A. and Lloyd G. Schermer; page 21: McLoughlin Bros., publisher/Library of Congress; page 23: Thanhouser Company/Wikimedia Commons; page 25: The Gilder Lehrman Institute, GLC00708; page 25: Library of Congress; page 26: National Park Service; page 28: © Tony Fischer/Flilckr.com (CC BY 3.0); page 30: © MARKA/Alamy Stock Photo

Copyright © 2024 by Cherry Lake Publishing Group

All rights reserved. No part of this book may be reproduced or utilized in any form or by any means without written permission from the publisher.

Cherry Lake Press is an imprint of Cherry Lake Publishing Group.

Library of Congress Cataloging-in-Publication Data has been filed and is available at catalog.loc.gov.

Cherry Lake Publishing Group would like to acknowledge the work of the Partnership for 21st Century Learning, a Network of Battelle for Kids. Please visit http://www.battelleforkids.org/networks/p21 for more information.

Printed in the United States of America
Corporate Graphics

Note from publisher: Websites change regularly, and their future contents are outside of our control. Supervise children when conducting any recommended online searches for extended learning opportunities.

Samantha Bell was born and raised near Orlando, Florida. She grew up in a family of eight kids and all kinds of pets, including goats, chickens, cats, dogs, rabbits, horses, parakeets, hamsters, guinea pigs, a monkey, a raccoon, and a coatimundi. She now lives with her family in the foothills of the Blue Ridge Mountains, where she enjoys hiking, painting, and snuggling with their cats Pocket, Pebble, and Mr. Tree-Tree Triggers.

CONTENTS

Chapter 1:
The Story People Tell: Saving Smith | 4

Chapter 2:
The Facts of the Matter: Between Two Streams | 10

Chapter 3:
Spinning the Story: A Self-Serving Fiction | 18

Chapter 4:
Writing History: Recognizing Bias | 24

Activity: Comparing Stories | 30
Learn More | 31
Glossary | 32
Index | 32

CHAPTER 1

The Story People Tell

Saving Smith

The lands that make up the United States had many different names in the past. Tsenacommacah (sen-uh-KAHM-uh-kuh) was one such name. Tsenacommacah stretched from present-day North Carolina to southern Maryland. **Algonquian** peoples lived there, including the Powhatan, Pamunkey, and Mattaponi. More than 30 Algonquian-speaking nations made up Tsenacommacah. Together, the nations were known as the Powhatan Nation. Chief Powhatan Wahunsenaca was **paramount** chief.

This Chesapeake Bay region is called Werowocomoco, or "place of leadership," and was the capital of the Powhatan Chiefdom.

In 1607, a ship from England arrived. Sailors and soldiers had sailed from England to start a colony. They built Jamestown, the first permanent English settlement in North America. The colony was built to increase England's power and wealth. Conflicts and fights broke out between the Powhatan people and the people in Jamestown. The groups attempted to make peace several times. One of Chief Powhatan's daughters played an important role. This is the story people tell about her.

The story says that her name was Pocahontas and she was very beautiful. Pocahontas enjoyed a peaceful life with her people. But everything was about to change. The story says that in 1607, as Pocahontas was walking along the shore, she spotted a large, strange boat in the distance. She hid among the trees, watching as the boat came closer. She heard voices shouting in a different language. Then she saw people in strange clothes come ashore. English men

Jamestown began as a fort. This 1950s painting by Sidney E. King shows the sailors and soldiers building Fort James in 1607.

and boys had arrived to start a settlement. It became known as the Jamestown Colony of Virginia.

For many days, Pocahontas watched them from the safety of the forest. Some were working on building a fort, while others went exploring. One of the explorers was a tall, handsome man. The others called him John Smith. He bravely led the group as they searched the new land. For a while, Pocahontas admired Smith from far away. The story says that eventually they met and fell in love.

But Pocahontas' father had also heard about the newcomers. He did not trust them. He ordered his warriors to bring their leader to him. They captured John Smith and took him to their village. After many days, Chief Powhatan decided that Smith should be executed. They forced him to the ground with his face against the dirt. Chief Powhatan picked up a huge club. He held it high over his head. The story says that just as he was about to hit Smith, Pocahontas threw

ACROSS THE SEA

At first, Jamestown faced many struggles, including disease and starvation. The men were spending their time searching for gold instead of planting crops. They sent back shipments of fool's gold, or pyrite, which is all they found. But under Smith's leadership, the colony began to grow. Then one night, he was injured in a mysterious gunpowder explosion. His injury was so severe that he had to return to England for treatment. He left Jamestown in October 1609. Smith was never able to sail to Virginia again. The colonists told Pocahontas and her father that Smith had died. She was surprised to see him again several years later in England.

Artists have recreated the fictional event of Pocahontas saving John Smith many times. This drawing is from 1870.

herself over Smith. She put herself between Smith and the deadly blow. The chief froze and stared at his daughter. Slowly, he lowered the club. His men untied Smith and let him go. Pocahontas' brave act had saved Smith's life. Still, Smith had to return to England and the two never saw each other again.

People tell this story to show how welcome the English colonists were. They share the story to tell how people from different cultures have things in common. But this story is not true. It was made up. The real story is one of greed, theft, and kidnapping.

CHAPTER 2

The Facts of the Matter

Between Two Streams

The real story of Pocahontas is one of courage, loss, and great change. She was born around 1596. Pocahontas was not the name she was born with. Her birth name was Amonute. She was also named Matoaka, "flower between two streams." She may have been born between the Mattaponi and Pamunkey rivers. She was born between two peoples as well. Her father, Wahunsenaca, was Pamunkey. Her mother was Mattaponi.

Amonute's mother died in childbirth. Her mother's name was Pocahontas. As Amonute grew up, she reminded people of her mother. They called her Pocahontas, too.

Amonute had many brothers and sisters. But she was her father's favorite. As she grew, she would have been busy

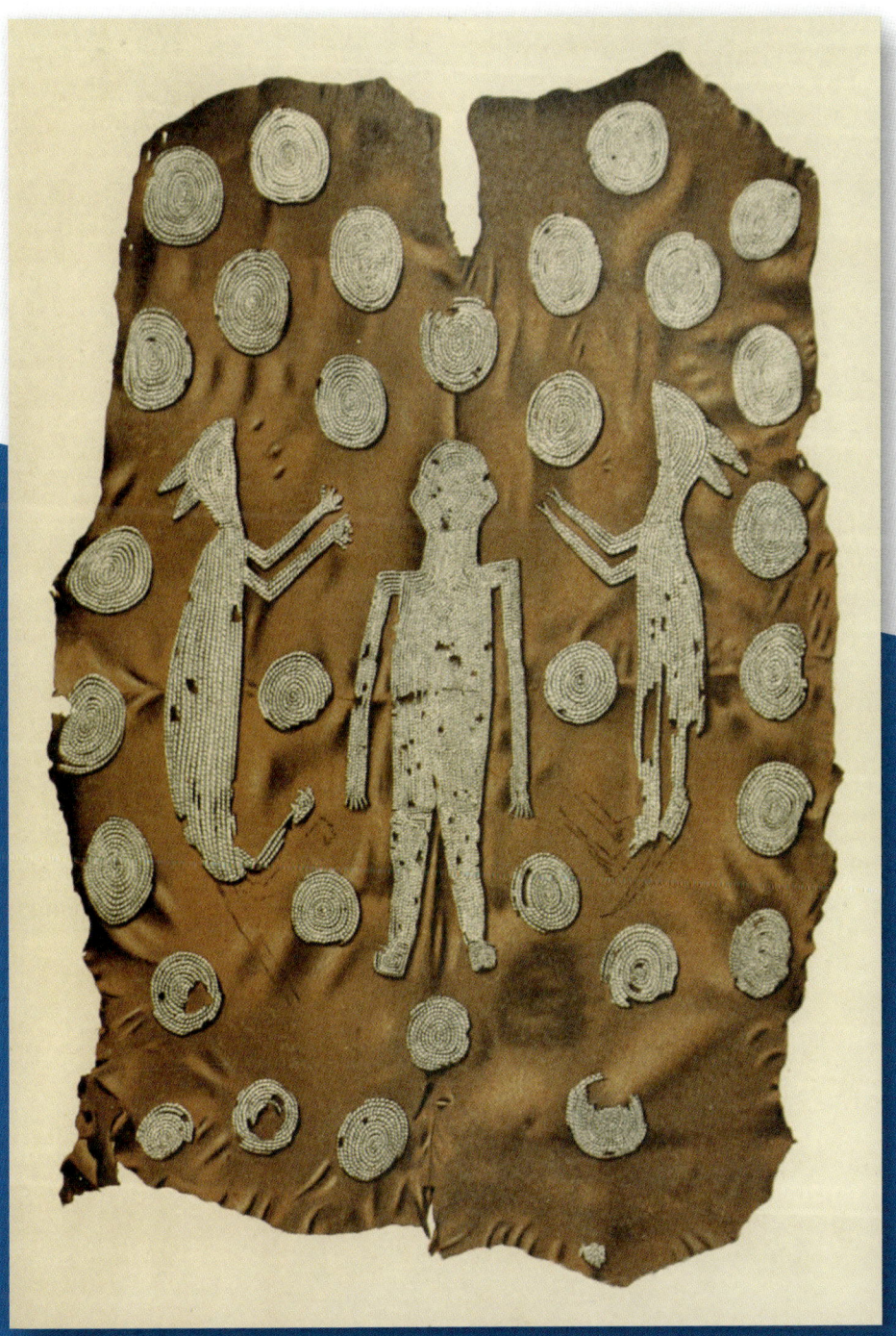

Chief Powhatan Wahunsenaca's deerskin and shell mantle is in the Ashmolean Museum in England. Artifacts like this help tell the real story of history.

Powhatan towns included large farms where women grew crops such as corn, squash, and beans.

learning to do women's work. This included building houses, farming, and cooking. Amonute would have learned to make mats, baskets, pots, and spoons. She would have prepared animal skins to make clothing. She would have also learned how to identify and use plants.

When the English arrived in May 1607, Amonute was only about 10 or 11 years old. The English colonists visited Powhatan towns. Some records say they traded for food. Mattaponi history says colonists like John Smith stole the food at gunpoint.

A few months after the English arrived, a group of Powhatan captured John Smith. The group was led by Chief Powhatan's younger brother and chief of the Pamunkey, Opechancanough. Smith was brought to meet Chief Powhatan. Smith's notes from that year describe their conversation. Chief Powhatan wanted to know why Smith and his people were there. The chief also wanted Smith to work for him and make things for him. Chief Powhatan learned that the English were starving. They needed food to survive in Jamestown.

Chief Powhatan grew to like Smith. He named him the werowance, or leader, of the colonists. A werowance was a special role. It was a chief or commander. Werowances were loyal to the paramount chief, Chief Powhatan, and paid him taxes. Honoring someone as a werowance involves a ceremony. Smith likely did not understand what was happening. Later in life, he described the ritual as an attempt to kill him. After being named a werowance, Smith was allowed to leave the village.

Powhatan *yehakhins* were single-family homes. These models are part of the re-created Powhatan Indian Village at the Jamestown Settlement in Jamestown, Virginia.

Smith returned to Jamestown. Chief Powhatan began sending them gifts of food. He sent Amonute and others with the gifts as a sign of peace. But as time passed, the relationship between the Powhatan and the settlers began to break down. In the winter of 1608 to 1609, the settlers needed more corn. They went to various tribes to try to trade beads and other trinkets for food. But a severe **drought** had reduced the tribes' harvests as well. They had little food to spare. The settlers threatened the tribes and burned their villages to get food. About this time, Smith was injured and returned to England. Amonute stopped visiting the fort.

By this time, Amonute was considered an adult. People still debate what her life was like. Even Indigenous stories differ. One possibility is as follows. Amonute may have chosen the name Pocahontas as her adult name. It honored her mother. Pocahontas, now around 14, may have married a warrior named Kocoum. Kocoum was the son of one of her father's werowances. Pocahontas and Kocoum would have moved to Kocoum's village, Potowomac. They may have had a son. Mattaponi history says they did, and his name was Little Kocoum.

In 1613, English Captain Samuel Argall wanted to make Jamestown richer. He wanted to force the Powhatan people to do what he wanted. He threatened Kocoum's brother, the chief. They tricked Pocahontas onto Argall's boat.

LITTLE KOCOUM'S LEGACY

Pocahontas would never have seen her son again after her kidnapping. Mattaponi history says that Little Kocoum was raised by Mattaponi women. He grew up and had children of his own. Some Indigenous families claim to be **descendants** of Little Kocoum. Wayne Newton, a famous entertainer, is from one such family.

Pocahontas's marriage and conversion to Christianity came after years of captivity.

Argall captured Pocahontas. Colonists likely killed Kocoum. Argall held Pocahontas for **ransom**. He demanded Chief Powhatan return stolen weapons and English prisoners.

Chief Powhatan met many of the demands. But Argall did not let Pocahontas go. Instead, the English settlers told her that her father no longer loved her. She remained a prisoner for 2 years. During that time, she learned the English ways of life. She learned about the Christian religion and changed her name to Rebecca. Mattaponi history tells of Pocahontas's depression. Her sister Mattachanna came to be with her. In 1614, Chief Powhatan agreed to a marriage between Pocahontas and a colonist named John Rolfe. Pocahontas had a son named Thomas. Once married, the Powhatan shared tobacco drying techniques with Rolfe. Tobacco became popular in England. Jamestown grew richer.

In 1616, Pocahontas, Rolfe, and Thomas traveled to England. They were to help create interest in Jamestown so more people would settle there. Pocahontas and Rolfe were in England for 10 months. She was presented as a **"civilized"** Native American. She even met the king and queen of England. In March 1617, the family planned to return to Virginia. But right before they left, Pocahontas became very sick. Soon after, she died. Mattachanna said she was healthy before a meal. Some believe Pocahontas was poisoned. She was only about 21 years old. Her Powhatan family wanted her body returned home. Instead, she was buried in a cemetery at St. George's Church in Gravesend, England. But in 1787, the church burned down. Today, no one knows the exact location of her grave.

CHAPTER 3

Spinning the Story
A Self-Serving Fiction

The story of Pocahontas has been told and retold many times. The characters in the story usually remain the same. But their actions or motivations are often different. One reason is because there are only a few historical records about Pocahontas. Much of what historians know come from letters and other writings by English colonists. It is only recently that the Mattaponi and Pamunkey histories have been included in the retellings.

John Smith was one of the first to **misrepresent** Pocahontas. He wrote about Pocahontas saving him from being killed by her father. He describes what sounds like a werowance ceremony, a place where a young child would not have been. He told how she was willing to sacrifice herself for him. This was because of her **compassionate** nature.

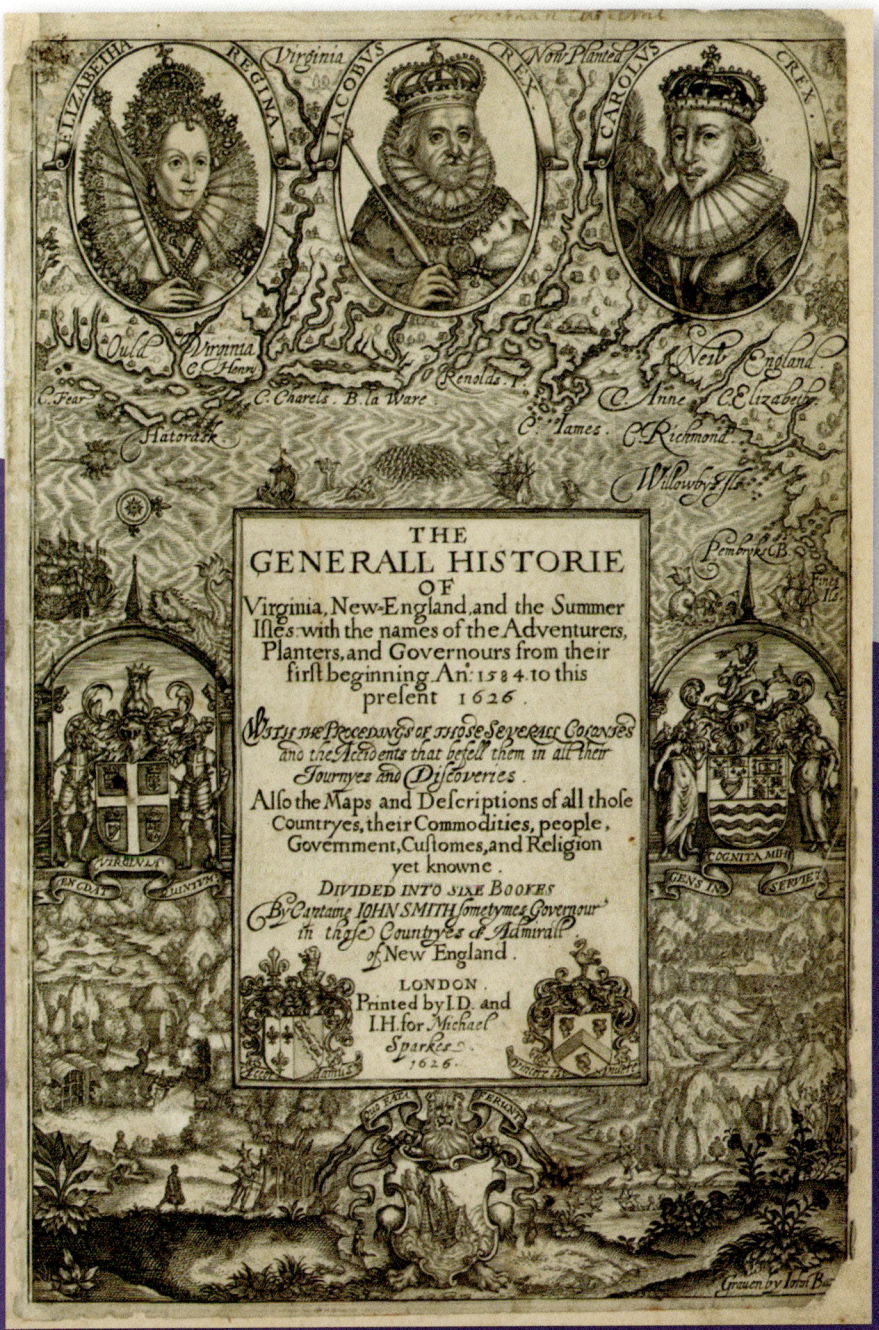

This is the title page from the 1626 edition of Smith's book *The Generall Historie of Virginia, New-England, and the Summer Isles*. His book created the fiction of Pocahontas.

Pocahontas's conversion to Christianity and her English marriage were used to justify colonialism.

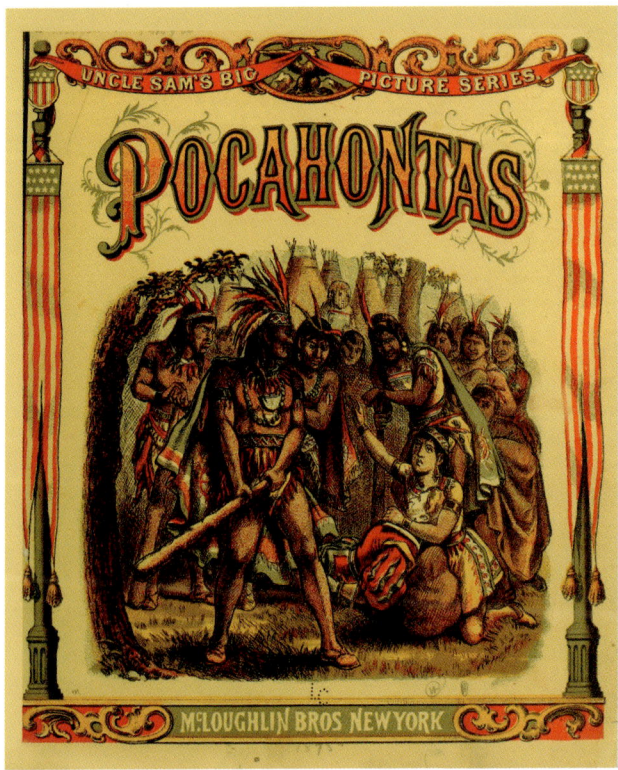

This children's book was published in 1873. It repeats John Smith's fiction and describes the Powhatan with prejudice.

But there is no reason to believe the event ever happened. Even later, John Smith wrote that Pocahontas was in love with him, which also was not true.

Pocahontas's story changed depending on when it was told. For example, in the 18th century, many people viewed Native Americans as fierce, violent, or wild. But to them, Pocahontas was different. She learned English and became a Christian. Stories and poems show her as civilized compared to the rest of her people. A poem called "Pocahontas" by Lydia H. Sigourney was especially popular. She published it in 1841. In the poem, Sigourney describes Pocahontas as a noble maiden who fits in with European society.

Movies about Pocahontas also added to the myth. One of the most well-known is the Disney cartoon. It was released in 1995. In the movie, Pocahontas is a woman about 20 years old. She is not a young girl. When she needs advice, she asks the old tree called Grandmother Willow. As the

POCAHONTAS IN BLACK AND WHITE

The first two movies about Pocahontas were made in the early 1900s. Both movies were short **silent films**. The first was *Pocahontas: Child of the Forest* in 1907. While it shows a scene of Pocahontas saving John Smith, it also adds to the story. It includes a Native American who is jealous of Smith and tries to kill him. The second film was released in 1910. It was called *Pocahontas*. It was based on the poem by Lydia Sigourney. Some people praised it for sticking so closely to the legend. Other reviews pointed out how it did not line up with historical facts, such as the clothing worn at the time.

Actress Anna Rosemond played the lead in the 1910 silent film Pocahontas. The film is presumed lost, but reviews and descriptions survived, including this still from the movie.

movie goes on, Pocahontas meets John Smith, and they fall in love. The movie includes the famous scene where Pocahontas saves Smith. It includes the warrior Kocoum. It has Pocahontas choosing Smith over Kocoum. While the cartoon is entertaining for many children, it does not show Pocahontas as she really was. Instead, it gives children a false picture of both her and the Jamestown colonists.

These stories spin a tale that makes the Jamestown colonists out to be kind and justified in their actions. It shows the Powhatan people as primitive and violent. It ignores the violence and cruelty inflicted on Pocahontas and her people. It ignores the stolen food and kidnapping as well as the possibly murdered husband and lost child.

CHAPTER 4

Writing History

Recognizing Bias

Historians use many types of records to put the pieces of the past together. Some are written accounts, such as journals and letters. Historians also use oral histories. These are collections of historical information passed down by word of mouth. To discover who Pocahontas really was, historians have had to use both. They have to be able to recognize **bias**, or unfair treatment for or against something.

John Smith wrote about his experiences at Jamestown in several books. Smith wanted to be remembered as a great adventurer. He wanted to make himself look good. He made himself sound brave and clever. He made himself sound like a hero. In his writings, Smith talked about being kidnapped by the Powhatan a few months after he arrived. While he was a prisoner, he met Pocahontas, the chief's daughter. He wrote about his injuries and near-death experiences. He used these

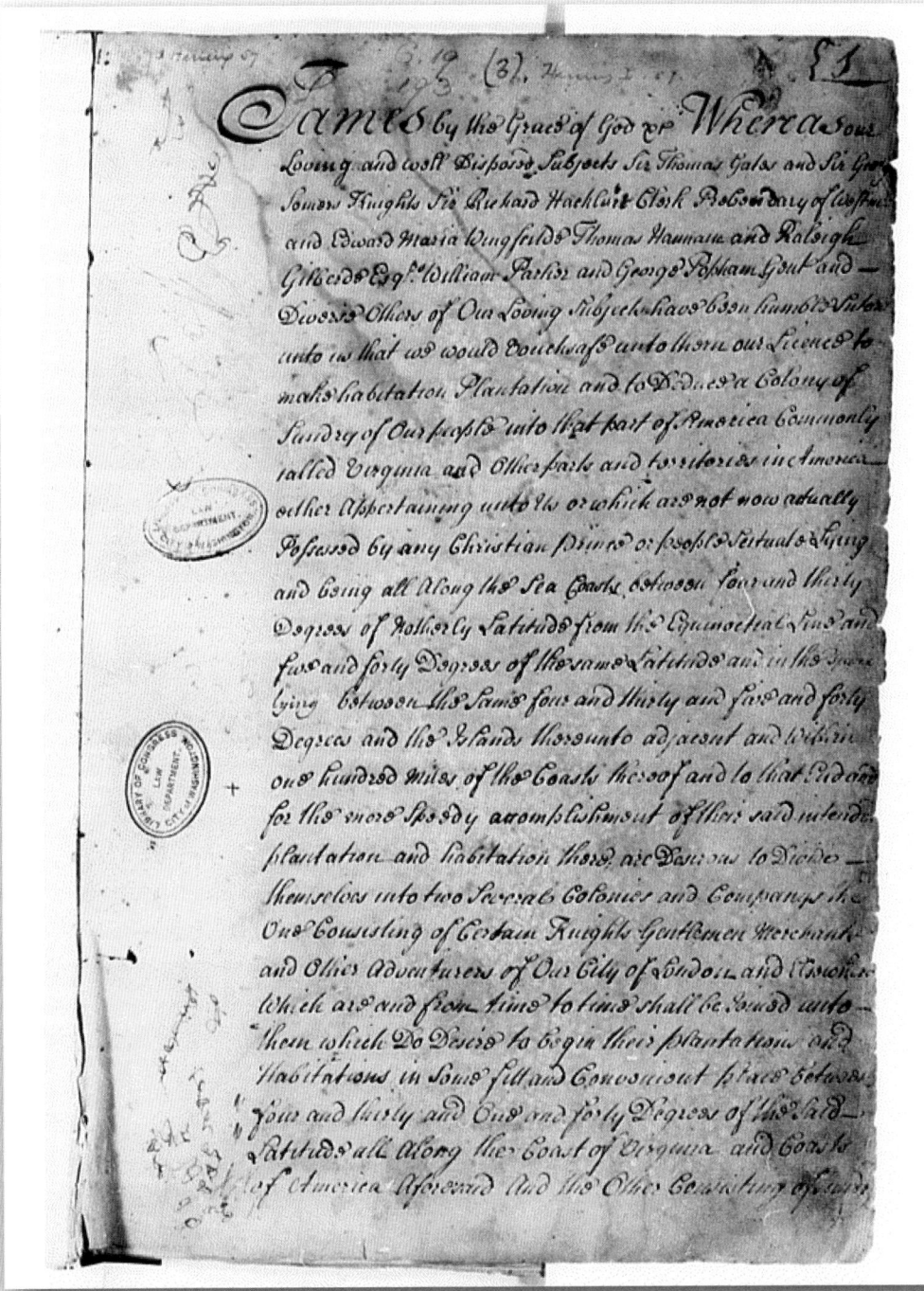

British records, like this Virginia Company charter, as well as letters and journals from colonists, help historians separate fact from fiction.

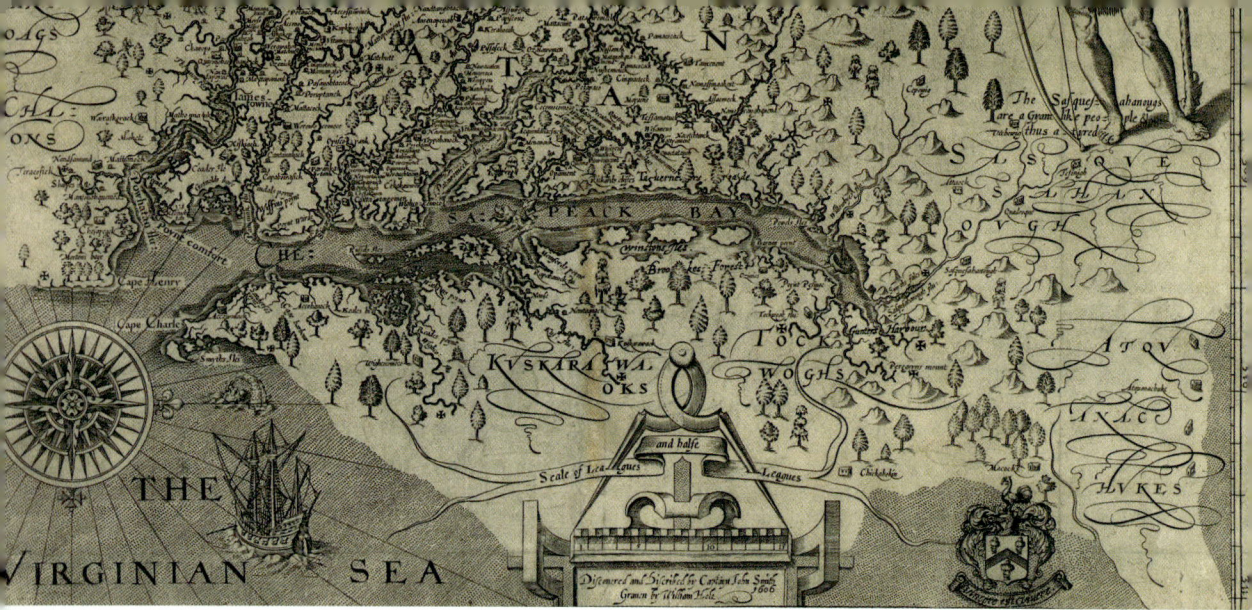

John Smith's map of the Chesapeake Bay area was used as a reference for many years.

events to support his image of a determined, fearless explorer. Although Smith exaggerated his actions, historians have verified that at least some of his information about Jamestown is correct. The rest shows his bias for himself.

Smith also wrote about Pocahontas. For example, in 1616, he wrote a letter to Queen Anne of Great Britain. In the letter, he described her character in detail. He talks about how he met her when she was a girl. He told the queen that Pocahontas was compassionate and brave. When relations with the Powhatans began to break down, Smith claimed that Pocahontas saved

Smith's life again. He said that her father had devised a plan to ambush Smith and his men. But Pocahontas sneaked through the woods and warned them in time. Smith told the queen that Pocahontas was the reason many settlers survived. None of this happened, but people believed John Smith. He had power and influence. His fiction was believed to be fact.

Another source of information about Pocahontas is her husband, John Rolfe. Through his letters, historians learned more about Pocahontas when she was older. For example, Rolfe wrote a letter to the deputy governor of Virginia. In this letter, Rolfe tells how Pocahontas **converted** to Christianity. He also asks for permission to

LEARNING TOGETHER

John Smith said he was held prisoner by Chief Powhatan for about 6 weeks. Historians know that he spent time with Pocahontas while he was there. Some evidence shows that they were teaching each other how to speak their languages. For example, historians have found notes written by Smith. They include sentences such as, "Tell Pocahontas to bring me three baskets." Another note says, "Pocahontas has many white beads."

This statue of Pocahontas was made in 1913 and stands in Historic Jamestown.

marry her. In another letter, Rolfe describes Pocahontas's arrival in England. He tells of the good impression she made on the English royal court. Other information about Pocahontas in England was written by some of the people she met there. Many of these sources were biased against Indigenous people. They did not think Indigenous people were as important as Europeans.

Pocahontas and her people spoke Algonquian. This language did not have a written form at the time. Today, it does. Still, there are firsthand accounts by the Mattaponi and Pamunkey. They passed these accounts down through the generations as oral histories. Mattaponi history tells how Pocahontas used to tear off English clothes because they were uncomfortable. It tells us that in England, Pocahontas saw John Smith and yelled at him for betraying the Powhatan. Her sister, Mattachanna, carried Pocahontas's story back home with her. Indigenous historians disagree on things as well. Different oral histories might contradict each other. Historians have to look at all perspectives to piece together the past.

Activity
Comparing Stories

Some people have criticized the Disney cartoon about Pocahontas because of the historical errors. Take some time to view the movie. As you are watching it, write down all the errors you see. When the film is over, look over your list. Do you think the movie was accurate enough? Why or why not? Write a paragraph explaining your answer.

Learn More

Books

Donaghey, Reese. *Pocahontas and the Powhatans.* New York, NY: Gareth Stevens Publishing, 2015.

Doyle, Abby Badach. *Pocahontas.* New York, NY: Enslow Publishing, 2023.

Rajczak, Kristen. *The Life of Pocahontas.* New York, NY: PowerKids Press, 2017.

Rusick, Jessica. *Living in the Jamestown Colony: A This or That Debate.* North Mankato, MN: Capstone Press, 2020.

On the Web

With an adult, explore more with these suggested searches.

"How Pocahontas Redefined How Europeans Saw Native Americans," World History Encyclopedia

"Pocahontas," America's Library

"Who Was Pocahontas?" American Revolution Museum at Yorktown

"Who Was the Real Pocahontas?" BBC Homeschool History

Glossary

Algonquian (al-GAHN-kwee-uhn) belonging to a group of North American languages once spoken from the Atlantic coast to the Great Lakes and the Great Plains

bias (BYE-uhs) an opinion or presentation of facts that is unfairly for or against something or someone

civilized (SIH-vuh-lyzd) educated and refined

compassionate (kuhm-PAH-shuh-nuht) kind and sympathetic

converted (kuhn-VUHR-tuhd) accepted different religious beliefs

descendants (dih-SEHN-duhnts) people who come from a certain ancestor

drought (DROWT) an unusually long time without rain

misrepresent (mis-reh-prih-ZENT) to describe something in an untrue or misleading way

paramount (PAIR-uh-mownt) supreme, most important

ransom (RAN-suhm) the payment demanded for the return of a prisoner

silent films (SYE-luhnt FILMZ) movies with no recorded sound

Index

activities, 30
Algonquian nations, 4, 29
Amonute. *See* Pocahontas
Argall, Samuel, 15–16
artifacts, 11

bias, 21–22, 23, 24–27, 29

Chesapeake Bay, 5, 26

English colonialism and colonists, 6–9, 12–17, 18–23, 24–27, 29

films, 22–23, 30
food, 12, 13, 14, 23

historical documents, 18, 19, 24–27, 29

Jamestown colony (Virginia), 6–9, 12–14, 15–17, 23, 24–27, 28
kidnapping, 15–16, 23, 24
Kocoum, 15, 23

languages, 27, 29
letters, 18, 24, 26–27, 29

literature and film, 18–19, 21–23, 30
Little Kocoum, 15, 29

maps, 26
Mattachanna, 16, 17, 29
Mattaponi peoples. *See* Powhatan Nation

Newton, Wayne, 15

Opechancanough, 12–13
oral histories, 24, 29

Pamunkey peoples. See Powhatan Nation
Pocahontas
  art depictions, 9, 16, 17, 20, 23, 28
  biography and facts, 11–17, 24, 27
  myth and legend, 6–9, 18–23, 26–27, 30
"Pocahontas" (poem), 22
poetry, 22
Powhatan (chief)
  artifacts, 11
  biography and facts, 4, 11, 12–16, 29
  myth and legend, 6, 8–9, 18, 26–27

Powhatan Nation, 4–9, 11–15, 18, 21, 23, 26–27, 29
primary sources
  artifacts, 11
  documents, 18, 24–27, 29

Rolfe, John, 16–17, 27, 29

Sigourney, Lydia H., 22
Smith, John
  art depictions, 13
  biography and facts, 12–14, 28, 29
  myth and legend, 7–9, 18, 20–21, 22–23, 24, 26–27, 30
  writings, 18–19, 21, 24, 26–27, 29
storytelling, 4–9, 20–25, 30

Tsenacommacah (land), 4

Wahunsenaca. *See* Powhatan (chief)
werowances, 13, 15, 18
Werowocomoco (land), 5

32